DiscoverRoo
An Imprint of Pop!
popbooksonline.com

History's Greatest Mysteries

HISTORY'S
SECRETS OF THE
AIR AND SEA

by Grace Hansen

abdobooks.com

Published by Pop!, a division of ABDO, PO Box 398166,
Minneapolis, Minnesota 55439. Copyright © 2023 by Abdo
Consulting Group, Inc. International copyrights reserved in all
countries. No part of this book may be reproduced in any form
without written permission from the publisher. DiscoverRoo™
is a trademark and logo of Pop!.

Printed in the United States of America, North Mankato,
Minnesota.

052022
092022

THIS BOOK CONTAINS
RECYCLED MATERIALS

Cover Photos: Shutterstock Images

Interior Photos: Shutterstock Images; Getty Images; AP Image
Collection

Editor: Elizabeth Andrews
Series Designer: Candice Keimig

Library of Congress Control Number: 2021951859

Publisher's Cataloging-in-Publication Data

Names: Hansen, Grace, author.

Title: History's secrets of the air and sea / by Grace Hansen

Description: Minneapolis, Minnesota : Pop, 2023 | Series:
History's greatest mysteries | Includes online resources
and index

Identifiers: ISBN 9781098242305 (lib. bdg.) | ISBN
9781098243005 (ebook)

Subjects: LCSH: Interactions of atmosphere and ocean--
Juvenile literature. | Aircraft accidents--Investigation-
-Juvenile literature. | Shipwrecks--Juvenile literature. |
Curiosities and wonders--Juvenile literature.

Classification: DDC 629.1309--dc23

WELCOME TO DiscoverRoo!

Pop open this book and you'll find QR codes loaded
with information, so you can learn even more!

Scan this code* and others
like it while you read, or visit
the website below to make
this book pop!

popbooksonline.com/secrets-air-sea

*Scanning QR codes requires a web-enabled smart device with a QR code reader app and a camera.

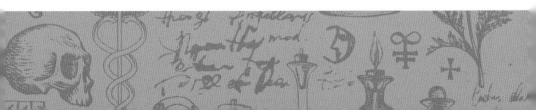

TABLE OF CONTENTS

CHAPTER 1

UNCHARTED TERRITORY

For humans, the last century and a half has been transformative. In 1903, we took our first flight in an airplane. In 1969, we walked on the moon. And yet, while we've used boats for thousands of years, just about five percent of the seafloor has

WATCH A VIDEO HERE!

Much of the ocean is too deep for humans to explore it.

been mapped, leaving most of Earth

unexplored. It's no wonder the sea and

the salty air just above the surface hold

so many secrets.

CHAPTER 2

THE GHOST SHIP

In 1868, the *Mary Celeste* was shined up, **refitted**, and had its new name. Once called *Amazon*, the ship had a shaky past. Its first captain died. It later ran aground in terrible winds. Some would say the ship was cursed. But that didn't bother the new owner. Captain Benjamin

LEARN MORE HERE!

Captain Briggs was a master sailor from Massachusetts.

Spooner Briggs was very proud of his new ship. He was ready to take the *Mary Celeste* on her next voyage from New York to Genoa, Italy. On November 7, 1872, Briggs, his wife, their two-year-old daughter, and the ship's crew weighed anchor and sailed into the open sea.

On December 5, from the deck of the *Dei Gratia*, Captain David Morehouse and seaman John Johnson spotted sails about five miles (8km) away. The ship looked unsteady, like it was in trouble. Captain Morehouse moved closer to

Luckily, the Dei Gratia's *lookout spotted the unmanned* Mary Celeste.

the ship. He got near enough to see the

vessel's name: *Mary Celeste*. He yelled to

it, but there was no response and no sign

of anyone on board. The captain sent

Johnson, Oliver Deveau, and John Wright

to inspect the ship.

"All hands to the pumps" is an emergency phrase with a nautical origin. It comes from when a leak in the ship's hull required help from the entire crew to bail out incoming seawater.

Deveau saw that there was water in the ship's hold, but the pumps were in good working order. There was plenty of drinking water and at least six months' worth of supplies. He also found that there were no lifeboats onboard and the compass was damaged. The men then spotted Briggs' **logbook**. The last entry was dated November 25 at 8:00 am. The entry for 9:00 am was blank.

An investigation into the *Mary Celeste*

and its missing crew went on for months.

The ship was closely examined. There

was no evidence that it had experienced

bad weather or any major damage. All

investigators knew was that something

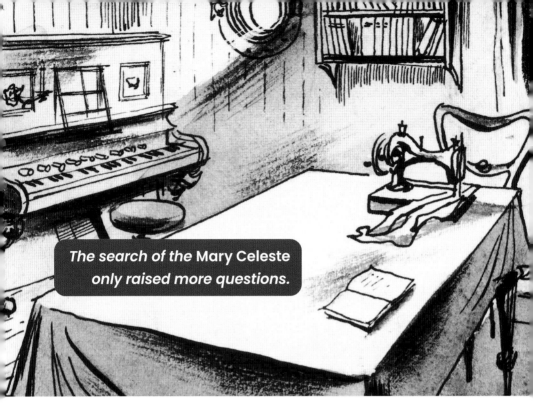

The search of the Mary Celeste only raised more questions.

disturbing enough happened for the

captain and crew to abandon ship,

and fast.

CHAPTER 3
X MARKS THE SPOT

Between 1716 and 1718, the **notorious**

pirate Blackbeard sailed the open seas.

For part of that time, he captained his

flagship the *Queen Anne's Revenge.*

Blackbeard and his nasty crew

mainly preyed on ships traveling from

Mexico and South America to Spain.

COMPLETE AN ACTIVITY HERE!

Blackbeard lit fuses in his hair that smoked. It made him look devilish and terrified his foes.

But Blackbeard wasn't interested in the ships themselves. He was concerned with the ships' **cargo holds**, which were packed full of gold, silver, and other treasures.

Using cannons to take over ships was an art. Pirates wanted a quick surrender without doing too much damage.

Blackbeard **plundered** until he was finally captured by the British naval force. Before his death, he was sure to note in his ledger that his vast treasure "lay in the location known only to him and the devil."

Everyone from treasure hunters to historians have wondered where Blackbeard buried his wealth. November

21, 1996, marks a day that searchers came one step closer to the answer. Archaeologist David Moore and members from the company Intersal Inc. located the *Queen Anne's Revenge* one mile off the coast of North Carolina. The wrecked ship rested on the ocean floor in 28 feet (8.5m) of water, her remaining cannons still loaded but rusting away.

EDWARD TEACH

Edward Teach was born in 1680 in England, likely to a respectable family. But by late 1716, Teach was better known as Blackbeard. He earned his pirate name for his lush black beard, which he often wore braided and tied with ribbons.

Since its discovery, more than 300,000 items have been recovered from the wreck. However, none of the artifacts amount to anywhere near what

One of the cannons of the Queen Anne's Revenge was raised from the wreck in June 2013.

The rusted anchor was pulled from the water in May 2011.

historians believe Blackbeard's treasure is worth. This is because Blackbeard ran the ship aground in June 1718, before his capture. All his stolen riches were then put on several smaller ships.

Where the treasure was stashed has been a mystery for more than three centuries. The loot could have ended up anywhere from Virginia to the Caribbean Islands. Perhaps one day, someone will stumble upon it.

Pirate William Kidd was from Scotland. He died in 1701 after burying his stolen riches in many locations. His hidden treasure could be worth millions today.

QUEEN ANNE'S REVENGE
FACTS AND FIGURES

TYPE: Frigate

LENGTH: 103 feet (31.4m)

CREW: Up to 300

WEAPONS AND ARMS: 40 Cannons

FIRST LAUNCHED: 1710

CAPTURED BY PIRATES: 1717

FATE: Ran aground in June of 1718 near Beaufort Inlet, North Carolina

CHAPTER 4

THE FINAL FLIGHT

Amelia Mary Earhart was born to fly.

The confident and charming girl from

Atchison, Kansas, had a fascination with

adventure. But it wasn't until Amelia was

23, in 1920, that she took her first plane

ride. Amelia said, "As soon as we left the

EXPLORE LINKS HERE!

ground, I knew myself I had to fly." At a time when women rarely worked outside the home, let alone piloted aircraft, Amelia's self-confidence and daring spirit served her well.

Aviator Amelia Earhart was known for remaining cool under pressure.

By 1922, Earhart had already accomplished what would be the first of many record-breaking flights. She flew her Airster plane to 14,000 feet (4,300m), higher than that type of plane had flown before. It took another 10 years for the entire world to know the name Amelia Earhart. In May 1932, Earhart became

Earhart in front of her Lockheed Electra.

the first woman to fly solo across the Atlantic Ocean.

In 1936, Earhart was ready for her most daring adventure yet. She would be the first woman to fly around the world. It took serious preparation, but on June 1, 1937, Earhart and **navigator** Fred Noonan squeezed into the small but powerful Lockheed Electra airplane. They took off from Miami, Florida, at 5:56 am to begin their globe-circling journey.

Fred Noonan was an American flight navigator. He also had a successful maritime career during WWI and after.

Besides a few weather delays and some technical issues, each **leg** had gone well. However, Earhart noted that she was not sleeping much and had a bad stomach. Nearing the end of the journey, Earhart and Noonan set off for

Howland Island on June 30. The *Itasca*, a US Coast Guard ship, waited near the island ready to support the flight as it neared. Unfortunately, the ship's radio operators were unaware Earhart and Noonan could not read **Morse code**, which was all they had used to communicate for hours.

Earhart felt at home in the cockpit.

Earhart shows the inflatable life raft that was onboard her flight around the world.

Finally, 19 hours into the flight, the *Itasca* heard from Earhart and Noonan. The radio operator logged the call: "We must be on you but cannot see you, but gas is running low. Have been unable to reach you by radio. We are flying at 1,000 feet (305m)." The ship and its crew saw no sign of the plane overhead. The Electra was off course.

Ships and planes scoured the area for days in search of Earhart, Noonan, and their aircraft. But there was no trace

of anyone or anything. In the decades

since the flight went

missing, expeditions

and **theories** as

to what happened

have amassed. Most

believe the Electra

ran out of fuel and

crashed, either into

the Pacific Ocean or

on a deserted island.

DESERTED ISLAND THEORY

In 1940, human remains were found on Gardner Island, now called Nikumaroro Island, which is about 400 miles southeast of Howland Island. The bones were sent to Fiji to be analyzed but were lost. More bone fragments were discovered on the same island in 2010, but DNA testing was inconclusive.

MAKING CONNECTIONS

TEXT-TO-SELF

Do you have any theories about the mysteries mentioned in this book? If so, what are they?

TEXT-TO-TEXT

Have you read any other books about mysterious events? What kind of information did you learn in those books that was not in this book?

TEXT-TO-WORLD

Do you think it is important for people to solve older mysteries concerning ships and aircraft? Why or why not?

GLOSSARY

cargo hold — the area on a ship where goods are stored.

leg — a specific distance in a journey.

logbook — any book for keeping records of events, navigation details, or the like.

Morse code — a code in which letters of the alphabet or numbers are presented by dots or dashes or by short and long flashes of light or sound.

navigator — a person who charts and sets the course of an aircraft.

notorious — known for something bad.

plunder — to loot or steal from by force.

refitted — made ready for use again.

theory — a reasonable and sometimes widely accepted explanation for something that happened.

INDEX

ONLINE RESOURCES
popbooksonline.com

Scan this code* and others like it while you read, or visit the website below to make this book pop!

popbooksonline.com/secrets-air-sea

*Scanning QR codes requires a web-enabled smart device with a QR code reader app and a camera.